Tatanka and the Lakota People

W9-ATM-940

Tatanka and the Lakota People

A Creation Story   Illustrated by Donald F. Montileaux

South Dakota

State Historical Society Press

Pierre, South Dakota

© 2006 by the South Dakota State Historical Society Press

All rights reserved.
This book or portions thereof in any form whatsoever may not
be reproduced without the expressed written approval of the
South Dakota State Historical Society Press, Pierre, S.Dak. 57501

The paintings in this book were originally commissioned by the
South Dakota State Historical Society for the *Oyate Tawicoh'an*
exhibit at the Cultural Heritage Center in Pierre, South Dakota. The
American Indian Advisory Committee for the exhibit selected the
traditional text that appears in this book. The committee's members
were: Martin Brokenleg, Tom Haukaas, Nellie Star Boy Menard,
Darlene Pipe Boy, Ben Rhodd, Shirley Sneve, Albert White Hat,
and Francis Whitebird. The Translation Committee for the exhibit
consisted of: Ben Black Bear, Jr., Earl Bullhead, Martina LaDeaux,
Nellie Star Boy Menard, Albert White Hat, and Francis Whitebird.

Production Date: May 2014
Plant and Location: Printed by Everbest Printing (Guangzhou,China)
Co. Ltd.,
Job and Batch #: 114285

This publication is funded in part by the
Great Plains Education Foundation.

Library of Congress Cataloging-in-Publication data
Tatanka and the Lakota people : a creation story / illustrated by
Donald F. Montileaux.
    p. cm.
  "The paintings in this book were originally commissioned by the
South Dakota State Historical Society for the Oyate Tawicoh'an
exhibit at the Cultural Heritage Center in Pierre, South Dakota"—T.p.
verso.
Includes bibliographical references.
ISBN-10 0-9749195-8-6 (cloth)
ISBN-13 978-0-9749195-8-4 (cloth)
ISBN-10 0-9822749-0-4 (paper)
ISBN-13 978-0-9822749-0-3 (paper)
1. Dakota mythology. 2. Creation—Mythology. I. Montileaux,
Donald F., 1948- II. South Dakota State Historical Society.
E99.D1T38 2006
398.2089'975243—dc22   200601600

Printed in China

18 17 16 15 14   7 8 9 10 11

Introduction

This story is one part of the Lakota creation legend. It tells how Tatanka—the buffalo—came to the Lakota people—the Ikce Wicasa of this story—so that they would have food and warmth. The full creation story is made up of many parts and is much longer. It also tells how the sky, the earth, and the sea came to be.

The Lakota people are American Indians from the Great Plains. They are often called the Sioux Indians. They have many important stories to tell. These narratives, which are told by the Lakota Elders, help Lakota children understand the world in which they live. The stories have been told and retold for many generations. Traditionally, the Elders passed legends down by word-of-mouth. Such storytelling is called oral history or *Ohunkakan* in Lakota. It has always been an important part of the Lakotas' lives. The details of the story can sometimes change depending on who tells the story and how often it is told, but the overall story remains the same from one storyteller to another and from one generation to the next. Many of these stories have now been written down so that more people can enjoy them.

The characters in this story also appear in other Lakota legends. Iktomi—or Spider, as he is sometimes known in English—has many tales told just about him. He is always a trickster, just as he is here. The Great Spirits, such as Skan, are also found in other legends. They control much of what happens in life. They were given names and shapes so that they would be easy to remember.

A Lakota artist—Donald Montileaux—painted the pictures for this book. His paintings capture the power of this story of creation with dramatic colors and bold shapes. At the end of the book, he tells more about how he made the paintings. The original Lakota words for this story are presented next to the English words. The translation of one language into another is never perfect. Words in different languages do not always equal each other precisely. Sometimes there is no perfect word to match another one, and people have to make the words fit as best as they can.

Tatanka and the Lakota People

The Great Spirit Skan, who grew out of Stone after the Earth was made, created our ancestors.

Taku skanskan inyan etan hinnape makoce ki kaga pi k'un hehan na he e ca unkaga pi.

He took our bones from Stone, our bodies from Earth, and our souls from himself and Wind and Thunder.

Hohu unkitawa pi ki inyan etan icu, tacan ki maka etanhan na nagi unkitawa pi ki iye etanhan na tate etan na wakinyan pi etanhan icu.

Sun warmed us.   Wi iyokal unyan pi.

Wisdom gave us intelligence.   Woksape wiyukcan unkiya pi.

Moon gave us affection.   Hanwi etan woyatan unkicu pi.

Revealer gave us longing
and love for children. All
their gifts gave us life.

Wayu'otan'in ki etan
wakanyeja unsiwicala pi na
awicayuhete pi ki he unkicu pi.

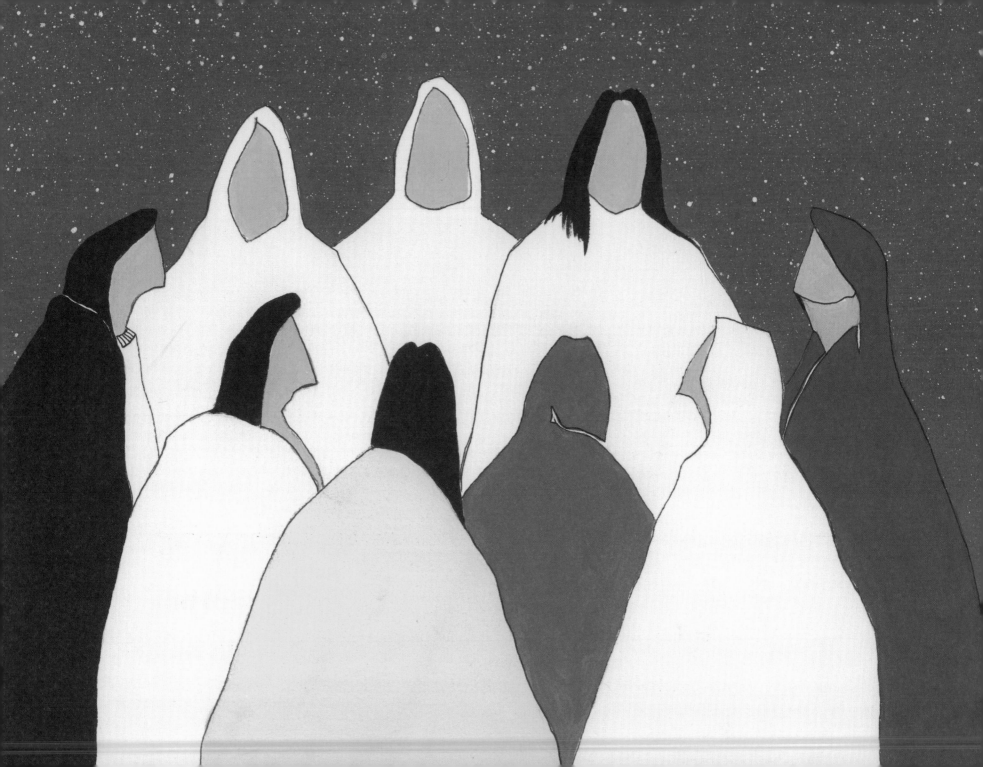

A council of the Spirits decided our purpose—to respect and care for the Spirits—and gave us our name—Pte Oyate—Buffalo Nation.

Wa'unk'u pi ki hena iyuha un unipi. Wakan okolakiciye ki he taku un ni unk'un pi ki he yustan pi – na pte oyate eya caje unyata pi.

After the nation had
lived for some time in the
Underworld,

Maka iyohlate otohanyan
pte oyate ki o'unyan pi wan
hehan.

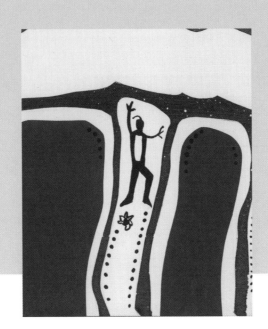

Spider, the Trickster, sent Wolf to the strongest young man in the nation.

Ikto sungmanitu tanka wan ekta yeyin na wicasa koskalaka wan ihankeya s'akeca ca ekta yekiye.

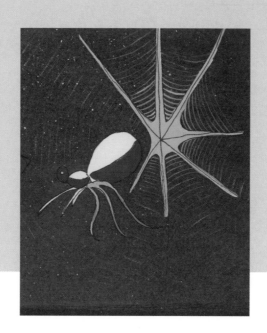

Wolf told this young man, Tokahe, that life would be easy on the surface of the earth.

Sungmanitu ki Tokahe okiyakin na maka akan hinapa pi hantans to'un pi ki ihankeya gluwaste pi kta keye.

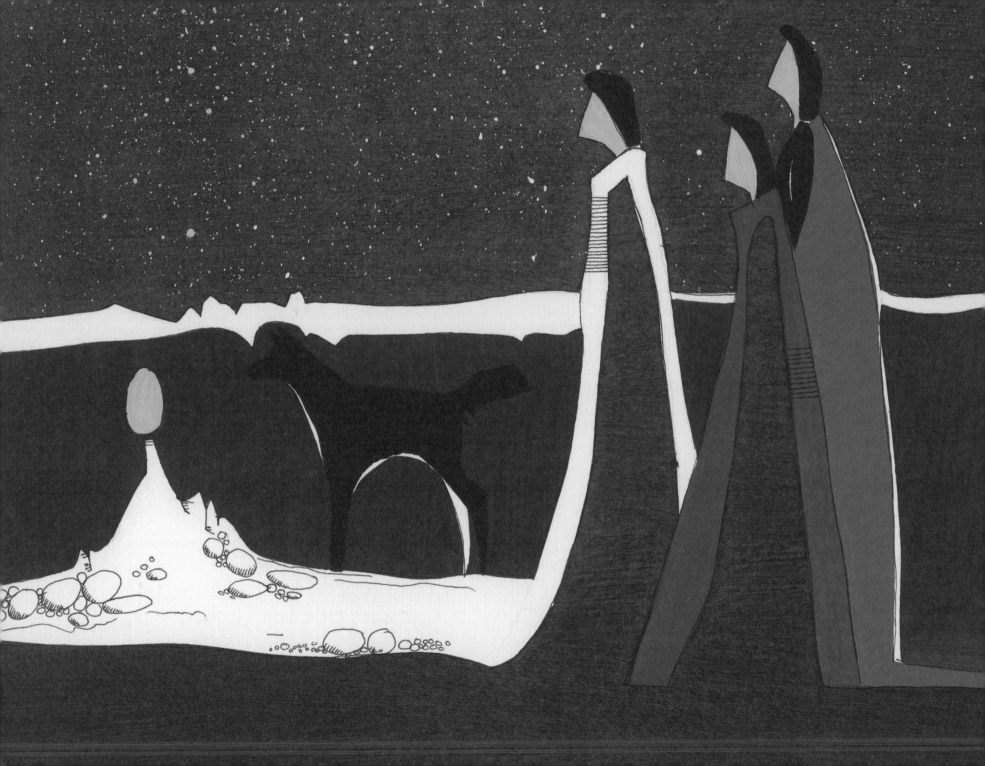

Tatanka, the holy man, warned Tokahe not to go to the surface. But Tokahe and the people did not listen. And so they found passage to the Black Hills through Wind Cave.

Tatanka, wicasa wakan ca Tokahe iwaktayin na hinape sni si. Eyas Tokahe e na toyate ki nah'un pi sni. Ho hecel He Sapa el wasun niyan wan ogna hinapa pi.

When the people found life on earth hard, Spider laughed at their folly.

Oyate makoce akan iyotiyekiya pi wan hehan Ikto awicahat'e.

But Tatanka, who had stayed in the Underworld, saw our nation in a vision.

Tatanka ektani maka mahel un ki oyate ki wo'ihanble un wanwicayanke.

We could not speak to the Spirits.
We had lost our language
and had to invent a new one.
We became Ikce Wicasa, the
Ordinary People.

Wanagi ob wo'unglaka pi
unkokihi pi sni. Iyapi ungnuni
pi ca iya pi lecala wan unkaga
pi hetan Ikce Wicasa he'uncapi.

To help us, Tatanka came to earth as a great, shaggy beast. He could speak directly with the Spirits.

Tatanka o'unkiya pi kta un maka akanl hi wamakaskan iyecel, na nagi etkiya wo'unkiciglaka pi okihi.

He was willing to give up his life
so we could have food, shelter,
and clothing.

Toni ki wa'unyekiya ca woyute
na oti na hayapi unyuha pi.

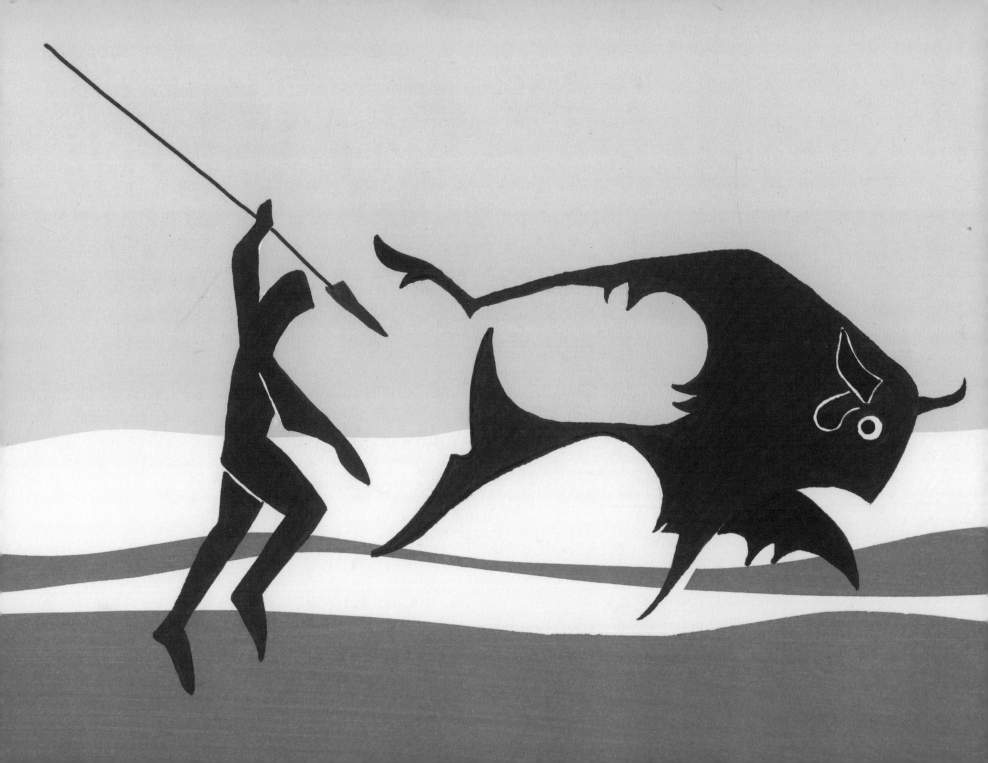

And so, from the beginning, Ikce Wicasa lived with the buffalo in the area around the Black Hills.

Hecetu un otokahe etanhan Ikce Wicasa ki tatanka ob He Sapa ita'oksan ni un pi.

A Note from the Illustrator

When I first started to research this story, I made a trip to Wind Cave in the Black Hills and walked around the entrance and the hole where the earth breathes. I had the story line and the information from my ancestors. I talked to people on the reservation and to other educators and artists. I was fortunate in the fact that I am an Oglala Lakota and from the Pine Ridge Indian Reservation in South Dakota. The Oglala Lakotas believe that we surfaced from Mother Earth through Wind Cave, where we were saved by the buffalo and grew strong as a people.

These illustrations are in a flat two-dimensional style that reflects the style of the traditional buffalo hides painted by my ancestors. I used this style in honor of my ancestors and found that it worked well in telling the story. The drawings compliment each other and, at the same time, each one can stand alone.

Donald F. Montileaux

Wind Cave

In American Indian stories, Wind Cave is often called the "hole that breathes cool air." This cave is near Buffalo Gap, South Dakota, and is now part of Wind Cave National Park in the southern Black Hills, a mountain range in South Dakota and Wyoming. Wind Cave is one of the largest and most complex caves in the world. Apart from strange winds, it features unique formations that look like honeycomb.

Further Reading

Lund, Bill. *The Sioux Indians*. Mankato, Minn.: Bridgestone Books, 1998.

Koestler-Grack, Rachel A. *The Sioux: Nomadic Buffalo Hunters*. Mankato, Minn.: Blue Earth Books, 2003.